Also by Mark Strand

THE STORY
OF OUR LIVES

THE STORY OF OUR LIVES

with

THE MONUMENT

and

THE LATE HOUR

Poems by MARK STRAND

Alfred A. Knopf   New York   2002

THIS IS A BORZOI BOOK
PUBLISHED BY ALFRED A. KNOPF

www.randomhouse.com/knopf/poetry

These three titles were originally published separately:
    The Story of Our Lives and *The Late Hour,* Atheneum;
    and *The Monument,* Ecco Press.

Library of Congress Cataloging-in-Publication Data
    Strand, Mark
    [Story of our lives]
    The story of our lives ; with, The monument & The late
    hour : poems / by Mark Strand.
    p.   cm.
    "The story of our lives", "The late hour", and "The monument"
    were originally published separately—Publisher's info.
    ISBN 0-375-70975-4 (alk. paper)
    I. Title: Story of our lives ; with, The monument & The late hour.
    II. Strand, Mark, [date] Monument.   III. Strand, Mark, [date] Late hour.
    IV. Title: Monument.   V. Title: Late hour.   VI. Title.
    PS3569.T69 S73 2002
    811'.54—dc21   2001038228

Manufactured in the United States of America
First Edition

Contents

THE STORY
OF OUR LIVES

I

Elegy for My Father

ELEGY FOR MY FATHER

(Robert Strand 1908–68)

1   *The Empty Body*

The hands were yours, the arms were yours,
But you were not there.
The eyes were yours, but they were closed and would not open.
The distant sun was there.
The moon poised on the hill's white shoulder was there.
The wind on Bedford Basin was there.
The pale green light of winter was there.
Your mouth was there,
But you were not there.
When somebody spoke, there was no answer.
Clouds came down
And buried the buildings along the water,
And the water was silent.
The gulls stared.
The years, the hours, that would not find you
Turned in the wrists of others.
There was no pain. It had gone.
There were no secrets. There was nothing to say.
The shade scattered its ashes.
The body was yours, but you were not there.
The air shivered against its skin.
The dark leaned into its eyes.
But you were not there.

2 Answers

Why did you travel?
Because the house was cold.
Why did you travel?
Because it is what I have always done between sunset and sunrise.
What did you wear?
I wore a blue suit, a white shirt, yellow tie, and yellow socks.
What did you wear?
I wore nothing. A scarf of pain kept me warm.
Who did you sleep with?
I slept with a different woman each night.
Who did you sleep with?
I slept alone. I have always slept alone.
Why did you lie to me?
I always thought I told the truth.
Why did you lie to me?
Because the truth lies like nothing else and I love the truth.
Why are you going?
Because nothing means much to me anymore.
Why are you going?
I don't know. I have never known.
How long shall I wait for you?
Do not wait for me. I am tired and I want to lie down.
Are you tired and do you want to lie down?
Yes, I am tired and I want to lie down.

3 Your Dying

Nothing could stop you.
Not the best day. Not the quiet. Not the ocean rocking.
You went on with your dying.
Not the trees

Under which you walked, not the trees that shaded you.
Not the doctor
Who warned you, the white-haired young doctor who saved you once.
You went on with your dying.
Nothing could stop you. Not your son. Not your daughter
Who fed you and made you into a child again.
Not your son who thought you would live forever.
Not the wind that shook your lapels.
Not the stillness that offered itself to your motion.
Not your shoes that grew heavier.
Not your eyes that refused to look ahead.
Nothing could stop you.
You sat in your room and stared at the city
And went on with your dying.
You went to work and let the cold enter your clothes.
You let blood seep into your socks.
Your face turned white.
Your voice cracked in two.
You leaned on your cane.
But nothing could stop you.
Not your friends who gave you advice.
Not your son. Not your daughter who watched you grow small.
Not fatigue that lived in your sighs.
Not your lungs that would fill with water.
Not your sleeves that carried the pain of your arms.
Nothing could stop you.
You went on with your dying.
When you played with children you went on with your dying.
When you sat down to eat,
When you woke up at night, wet with tears, your body sobbing,
You went on with your dying.
Nothing could stop you.
Not the past.

Not the future with its good weather.
Not the view from your window, the view of the graveyard.
Not the city. Not the terrible city with its wooden buildings.
Not defeat. Not success.
You did nothing but go on with your dying.
You put your watch to your ear.
You felt yourself slipping.
You lay on the bed.
You folded your arms over your chest and you dreamed of the world
without you,
Of the space under the trees,
Of the space in your room,
Of the spaces that would now be empty of you,
And you went on with your dying.
Nothing could stop you.
Not your breathing. Not your life.
Not the life you wanted.
Not the life you had.
Nothing could stop you.

4   *Your Shadow*

You have your shadow.
The places where you were have given it back.
The hallways and bare lawns of the orphanage have given it back.
The Newsboys Home has given it back.
The streets of New York have given it back and so have the streets of
Montreal.
The rooms in Belém where lizards would snap at mosquitos have
given it back.
The dark streets of Manaus and the damp streets of Rio have given it
back.
Mexico City where you wanted to leave it has given it back.

And Halifax where the harbor would wash its hands of you has given it back.

You have your shadow.

When you traveled the white wake of your going sent your shadow below, but when you arrived it was there to greet you. You had your shadow.

The doorways you entered lifted your shadow from you and when you went out, gave it back. You had your shadow.

Even when you forgot your shadow, you found it again; it had been with you.

Once in the country the shade of a tree covered your shadow and you were not known.

Once in the country you thought your shadow had been cast by somebody else. Your shadow said nothing.

Your clothes carried your shadow inside; when you took them off, it spread like the dark of your past.

And your words that float like leaves in an air that is lost, in a place no one knows, gave you back your shadow.

Your friends gave you back your shadow.

Your enemies gave you back your shadow. They said it was heavy and would cover your grave.

When you died your shadow slept at the mouth of the furnace and ate ashes for bread.

It rejoiced among ruins.

It watched while others slept.

It shone like crystal among the tombs.

It composed itself like air.

It wanted to be like snow on water.

It wanted to be nothing, but that was not possible.

It came to my house.

It sat on my shoulders.

Your shadow is yours. I told it so. I said it was yours.

I have carried it with me too long. I give it back.

5   *Mourning*

They mourn for you.
When you rise at midnight,
And the dew glitters on the stone of your cheeks,
They mourn for you.
They lead you back into the empty house.
They carry the chairs and tables inside.
They sit you down and teach you to breathe.
And your breath burns,
It burns the pine box and the ashes fall like sunlight.
They give you a book and tell you to read.
They listen and their eyes fill with tears.
The women stroke your fingers.
They comb the yellow back into your hair.
They shave the frost from your beard.
They knead your thighs.
They dress you in fine clothes.
They rub your hands to keep them warm.
They feed you. They offer you money.
They get on their knees and beg you not to die.
When you rise at midnight they mourn for you.
They close their eyes and whisper your name over and over.
But they cannot drag the buried light from your veins.
They cannot reach your dreams.
Old man, there is no way.
Rise and keep rising, it does no good.
They mourn for you the way they can.

6   *The New Year*

It is winter and the new year.
Nobody knows you.

Away from the stars, from the rain of light,
You lie under the weather of stones.
There is no thread to lead you back.
Your friends doze in the dark
Of pleasure and cannot remember.
Nobody knows you. You are the neighbor of nothing.
You do not see the rain falling and the man walking away,
The soiled wind blowing its ashes across the city.
You do not see the sun dragging the moon like an echo.
You do not see the bruised heart go up in flames,
The skulls of the innocent turn into smoke.
You do not see the scars of plenty, the eyes without light.
It is over. It is winter and the new year.
The meek are hauling their skins into heaven.
The hopeless are suffering the cold with those who have nothing to
    hide.
It is over and nobody knows you.
There is starlight drifting on the black water.
There are stones in the sea no one has seen.
There is a shore and people are waiting.
And nothing comes back.
Because it is over.
Because there is silence instead of a name.
Because it is winter and the new year.

II

The Room

THE ROOM

I stand at the back of a room
and you have just entered.
I feel the dust
fall from the air
onto my cheeks.
I feel the ice
of sunlight on the walls.
The trees outside
remind me of something
you are not yet aware of.
You have just entered.
There is something like sorrow
in the room.
I believe you think
it has wings
and will change me.
The room is so large
I wonder what you are thinking
or why you have come.
I ask you,
What are you doing?
You have just entered
and cannot hear me.
Where did you buy
the black coat you are wearing?
You told me once.
I cannot remember
what happened between us.
I am here. Can you see me?
I shall lay my words on the table

as if they were gloves,
as if nothing had happened.
I hear the wind
and I wonder what are
the blessings
born of enclosure.
The need to get away?
The desire to arrive?
I am so far away
I seem to be in the room's past
and so much here
the room is beginning
to vanish around me.
It will be yours soon.
You have just entered.
I feel myself drifting,
beginning to be
somewhere else.
Houses are rising
out of my past,
people are walking
under the trees.
You do not see them.
You have just entered.
The room is long.
There is a table in the middle.
You will walk
toward the table,
toward the flowers,
toward the presence of sorrow
which has begun to move
among objects,
its wings beating

to the sound of your heart.
You shall come closer
and I shall begin to turn away.
The black coat you are wearing,
where did you get it?
You told me once
and I cannot remember.
I stand at the back
of the room and I know
if you close your eyes
you will know why
you are here;
that to stand in a space
is to forget time,
that to forget time
is to forget death.
Soon you will take off your coat.
Soon the room's whiteness
will be a skin for your body.
I feel the turning of breath
around what we are going to say.
I know by the way
you raise your hand
you have noticed the flowers
on the table.
They will lie
in the wake of our motions
and the room's map
will lie before us
like a simple rug.
You have just entered.
There is nothing to be done.
I stand at the back of the room

and I believe you see me.
The light consumes the chair,
absorbing its vacancy,
and will swallow itself
and release the darkness
that will fill the chair again.
I shall be gone.
You will say you are here.
I can hear you say it.
I can almost hear you say it.
Soon you will take off your black coat
and the room's whiteness
will close around you
and you will move
to the back of the room.
Your name will no longer be known,
nor will mine.
I stand at the back
and you have just entered.
The beginning is about to occur.
The end is in sight.

SHE

To Bill and Sandy Bailey

She slept without the usual concerns,
the troubling dreams—the pets
moving through the museum,
the carved monsters, the candles
giving themselves up to darkness.
She slept without caring what she looked like,
without considering the woman
who would come or the men who would leave
or the mirrors or the basin of cold water.
She slept on one side, the sheets
pouring into the room's cold air,
the pillow shapeless, her flesh
no longer familiar. Her sleep
was a form of neglect.
She did nothing for days,
the sun and moon had washed up
on the same shore. Her negligee
became her flesh, her flesh became
the soft folding of air over the sheets.
And there was no night, nor any sign of it.
Nothing curled in the air
but the sound of nothing,
the hymn of nothing, the humming
of the room, of its past.
Her flesh turned from itself
into the sheets of light.
She began to wake; her hair spilled
into the rivers of shadow.
Her eyes half-open, she saw the man across the room,
she watched him and could not choose

between sleep and wakefulness.
And he watched her
and the moment became their lives
so that she would never rise or turn from him,
so that he would always be there.

IN CELEBRATION

You sit in a chair, touched by nothing, feeling
the old self become the older self, imagining
only the patience of water, the boredom of stone.
You think that silence is the extra page,
you think that nothing is good or bad, not even
the darkness that fills the house while you sit watching
it happen. You've seen it happen before. Your friends
move past the window, their faces soiled with regret.
You want to wave but cannot raise your hand.
You sit in a chair. You turn to the nightshade spreading
a poisonous net around the house. You taste
the honey of absence. It is the same wherever
you are, the same if the voice rots before
the body, or the body rots before the voice.
You know that desire leads only to sorrow, that sorrow
leads to achievement which leads to emptiness.
You know that this is different, that this
is the celebration, the only celebration,
that by giving yourself over to nothing,
you shall be healed. You know there is joy in feeling
your lungs prepare themselves for an ashen future,
so you wait, you stare and you wait, and the dust settles
and the miraculous hours of childhood wander in darkness.

TO BEGIN

He lay in bed not knowing how to begin.
His mind was unclear, and whatever he felt
faded into an aspect of something
he had known already. Maybe
someone could tell him what to do.
Maybe he could say what he wanted
in his own voice and still be surprised,
say, for example, that it was just before dawn,
that the moon was still a prisoner to stone,
that the sun called so faintly
only a few birds heard it
and they sang for the light
the way some men sing for bread.
If he could say it so that people
believed him, so that he believed it,
he would go on. He would begin
to believe that waking meant
casting his sleep back into the night.
Later, he could learn to say what he meant
without actually saying it.
But he lay in bed, powerless to begin.

He thought how he had always carried
darkness into day where it blazed
into a likeness of himself.
He had stood like a ghost in sunlight,
barely visible, in whose eyes
the trees, the windows, the vanishings
of a previous life became real again.
Maybe he could say that.

But to whom? And for what reason?
To whom could he say that to lose
is to lose something, that to lose
again and again is to have more
and more to lose, that losing is having?

There was no reason to get up.
Let the sun shine without him.
He knew he was not needed,
that his speech was a mirror, at best,
that once he had imagined his words
floating upwards, luminous and threatening,
moving among the stars, becoming the stars,
becoming in the end the equal of all the dead
and the living. He had imagined this
and did not care to again.
If only he could say something,
something that had the precision
of his staying in bed.
It took no courage, no special
recklessness to discredit silence.
He had tried to do it, but had failed.
He had gone to bed and slept.
The phrases had disappeared, sinking
into sleep, unwanted and uncalled for.

He stared at the ceiling
and imagined his breath shaping itself into words.
He imagined that he would go to the water and look down,
that he would see the shimmer of fish
over the ruinous coral
and watch them die in the shade of his image.
But he could never say that.

Maybe the world would lighten
and without thinking he would be able to lift
from his back the wings of night
and lift the stones from his teeth
and would be able to speak.
But he could not say that either.
He could do nothing but lie there
and wait for the sun to go down,
wait for the promise of stillness
that would be sent from his heart into the field,
and wait for it to return.
And later he would lie there
and pretend it was morning.
In the dark he would still be uncertain of how to begin.
He would mumble to himself; he would follow
his words to learn where he was.
He would begin.
And the room, the house, the field,
the woods beyond the field, would also begin,
and in the sound of his own voice beginning
he would hear them.

III

The Story of Our Lives

THE STORY OF OUR LIVES

To Howard Moss

1

We are reading the story of our lives
which takes place in a room.
The room looks out on a street.
There is no one there,
no sound of anything.
The trees are heavy with leaves,
the parked cars never move.
We keep turning the pages,
hoping for something,
something like mercy or change,
a black line that would bind us
or keep us apart.
The way it is, it would seem
the book of our lives is empty.
The furniture in the room is never shifted,
and the rugs become darker each time
our shadows pass over them.
It is almost as if the room were the world.
We sit beside each other on the couch,
reading about the couch.
We say it is ideal.
It is ideal.

2

We are reading the story of our lives
as though we were in it,

as though we had written it.
This comes up again and again.
In one of the chapters
I lean back and push the book aside
because the book says
it is what I am doing.
I lean back and begin to write about the book.
I write that I wish to move beyond the book,
beyond my life into another life.
I put the pen down.
The book says: *He put the pen down*
and turned and watched her reading
the part about herself falling in love.
The book is more accurate than we can imagine.
I lean back and watch you read
about the man across the street.
They built a house there,
and one day a man walked out of it.
You fell in love with him
because you knew he would never visit you,
would never know you were waiting.
Night after night you would say
that he was like me.
I lean back and watch you grow older without me.
Sunlight falls on your silver hair.
The rugs, the furniture,
seem almost imaginary now.
She continued to read.
She seemed to consider his absence
of no special importance,
as someone on a perfect day will consider
the weather a failure
because it did not change his mind.

You narrow your eyes.
You have the impulse to close the book
which describes my resistance:
how when I lean back I imagine
my life without you, imagine moving
into another life, another book.
It describes your dependence on desire,
how the momentary disclosures
of purpose make you afraid.
The book describes much more than it should.
It wants to divide us.

3

This morning I woke and believed
there was no more to our lives
than the story of our lives.
When you disagreed, I pointed
to the place in the book where you disagreed.
You fell back to sleep and I began to read
those mysterious parts you used to guess at
while they were being written
and lose interest in after they became
part of the story.
In one of them cold dresses of moonlight
are draped over the backs of chairs in a man's room.
He dreams of a woman whose dresses are lost,
who sits on a stone bench in a garden
and believes in wonders.
For her love is a sacrifice.
The part describes her death
and she is never named,
which is one of the things

you could not stand about her.
A little later we learn
that the dreaming man lives
in the new house across the street.
This morning after you fell back to sleep
I began to turn pages early in the book:
it was like dreaming of childhood,
so much seemed to vanish,
so much seemed to come to life again.
I did not know what to do.
The book said: *In those moments it was his book.*
A bleak crown rested uneasily on his head.
He was the brief ruler of inner and outer discord,
anxious in his own kingdom.

               4

Before you woke
I read another part that described your absence
and told how you sleep to reverse
the progress of your life.
I was touched by my own loneliness as I read,
knowing that what I feel is often the crude
and unsuccessful form of a story
that may never be told.
I read and was moved by a desire to offer myself
to the house of your sleep.
He wanted to see her naked and vulnerable,
to see her in the refuse, the discarded
plots of old dreams, the costumes and masks
of unattainable states.
It was as if he were drawn
irresistibly to failure.

It was hard to keep reading.
I was tired and wanted to give up.
The book seemed aware of this.
It hinted at changing the subject.
I waited for you to wake not knowing
how long I waited,
and it seemed that I was no longer reading.
I heard the wind passing
like a stream of sighs
and I heard the shiver of leaves
in the trees outside the window.
It would be in the book.
Everything would be there.
I looked at your face
and I read the eyes, the nose, the mouth . . .

5

If only there were a perfect moment in the book;
if only we could live in that moment,
we could begin the book again
as if we had not written it,
as if we were not in it.
But the dark approaches
to any page are too numerous
and the escapes are too narrow.
We read through the day.
Each page turning is like a candle
moving through the mind.
Each moment is like a hopeless cause.
If only we could stop reading.
He never wanted to read another book
and she kept staring into the street.

The cars were still there,
the deep shade of trees covered them.
The shades were drawn in the new house.
Maybe the man who lived there,
the man she loved, was reading
the story of another life.
She imagined a dank, heartless parlor,
a cold fireplace, a man sitting
writing a letter to a woman
who has sacrificed her life for love.
If there were a perfect moment in the book,
it would be the last.
The book never discusses the causes of love.
It claims confusion is a necessary good.
It never explains. It only reveals.

6

The day goes on.
We study what we remember.
We look into the mirror across the room.
We cannot bear to be alone.
The book goes on.
They became silent and did not know how to begin
the dialogue which was necessary.
It was words that created divisions in the first place,
that created loneliness.
They waited.
They would turn the pages, hoping
something would happen.
They would patch up their lives in secret:
each defeat forgiven because it could not be tested,

each pain rewarded because it was unreal.
They did nothing.

7

The book will not survive.
We are the living proof of that.
It is dark outside, in the room it is darker.
I hear your breathing.
You are asking me if I am tired,
if I want to keep reading.
Yes, I am tired.
Yes, I want to keep reading.
I say yes to everything.
You cannot hear me.
They sat beside each other on the couch.
They were the copy, the tired phantoms
of something they had been before.
The attitudes they took were jaded.
They stared into the book
and were horrified by their innocence,
their reluctance to give up.
They sat beside each other on the couch.
They were determined to accept the truth.
Whatever it was they would accept it.
The book would have to be written
and would have to be read.
They are the book and they are
nothing else.

INSIDE THE STORY

He never spoke much
but he began to speak even less.
And the chair in the living room was unsafe.
And the bed in the bedroom was never made.
And nothing was the same as it had been.
Still, he said he was happy.
He would look at the stars
and their distance confirmed what he felt.
If there was order, then he was a part of it;
if there was chaos, then it wasn't his fault.
He had no cause for anger.
When he spoke to his wife
the subject was always the same:
she would travel and see the world,
he would stay home and water the plants;
or, he would see the world and she
would water the plants.
Their lives continued.
She undressed in the dark bathroom.
He read a dull book in the kitchen.
Nothing changed until she admitted she loved him;
that night he slept in the living room,
alone, and had a dream.

2

He dreamed that he had gone,
and no one had seen him off.
Under the simple moon
the stones and bushes looked alike.
It was the end of summer and he could smell the grass
and feel the wind from the lake.
He loved farewells. He loved
not knowing where he was going,
and the dark and the deep wind driving him
farther and farther were like desire.
And if his enemies crouched in the moonlight,
he did not notice them,
nor did he notice the owl staring into his limbs,
nor feel the moth pressing against his ribs
as if he were the only light.
And he did not hear the cry that would always be with him,
that rose from his throat like a name
beginning to shape the sound of its being.
He wanted to learn the lessons of dark,
and he wanted the sheets of morning to take him in.
He wanted both, and woke
unable to say the one thing he would try to remember.

3

It was early.
She stood over him, offering him coffee.
She asked him what he was trying to say.
There was no way to tell her what he had not said.
His voice would fail to convey what it was,
and his silence would fail to suggest its absence.

He remembered the driving wind
and the way he waved into the dark
and how the distance kept welcoming him.
He wished she had not asked.
He imagined that he had wakened in the wrong house,
that he would leave, that he would go back.
And he drifted off to sleep.
If he had gone before, he did not know it now.
The clouds moving slowly over the lake,
the failed brilliance of daylight,
seemed too much a part of the present.
He went from field to field,
each one blank with possibility,
each one darkening with disappointment.
As he went he felt the acuteness of his passion.
He walked because he had to,
and when he looked up, the sky was empty
and the world seemed cleared of meaning.
Once again, he tried to say something,
but he awoke.

                    4

She stood over him.
She said she had watched him,
that he had been trying to say something.
He had nothing to say.
He lay on the couch with his eyes open.
Sometimes he did not know if he slept
or just thought about sleep. He knew
that he would lie down and the journey would begin.
If it was another life, it was not the one which lasted.
He would have to come back

and recapture what he had left.
He would offer himself as hostage
and the life he woke into would take him.
How long would it last?
When he closed his eyes, the clouds had gone,
the sun had turned everything white.
Even if he became less than he was and the terrain
became harsher, even if no trace remained
of his having been, he would keep going.
He felt he had given up the visible world,
that the sun had turned everything white to prepare his way.
He walked in the harsh light,
and when he stopped he discovered
he was standing beside someone who wore clothes like his
and whose face was like his own and who asked,
Where am I? Where am I going?
He tried to answer but the cloud of his voice would say nothing.
He wanted to know who the man was.
He tried to think of his name, but again he woke.

5

She watched him open his eyes
and asked him what he had said about a name.
He tried to remember where he was going.
Was he looking for someone?
The light came in the windows,
erasing the furniture, turning
the room white. He saw nothing.
And he remembered how she would dress and undress
and how he would wait in bed, watching her.
All night he would feel her beside him,
her breathing moved through his dreams

and shook him like nothing else.
He had traveled a great distance since then
and did not know where he was going.
She told him the coffee was getting cold.
He closed his eyes.
The journey was not what he wanted.
Each day was too long, and not long enough
to endure himself in. And there was nothing ahead.
The stranger had gone and there was
no lake or fields or woods.
The sun's brightness fell and he continued,
his ignorance shining, his failure
finding him out and leading him on.
Survival was motion and he could not stop.

6

She sat in a chair across the room, staring at him.
It was not a bad life, he thought
as he sipped the cold coffee
and she moved into a closer chair.
Still, he could not speak.
She would leave the room and change
into a cooler dress, a warmer dress.
She might even take a trip.
She leaned over him. She said she'd been watching him,
was there something he wanted to tell her?
He knew she would meet somebody.
He knew she would leave him.
He tried to tell her to stay but it was no use.
His mouth was dry and the sun was white
and he could not take another step.
He tried to call, but could not remember the name.

He stood in the absence of what he had known
and waited, and when he woke
the room was empty. The light had turned
and the chair she had sat in was covered with dust.
He had been gone a long time
and now the journey was over.
Without her he would not be able to sleep,
and there was no more to say,
and even if there were, he would not say it.

THE UNTELLING

He leaned forward over the paper
and for a long time saw nothing.
Then, slowly, the lake opened
like a white eye
and he was a child
playing with his cousins,
and there was a lawn
and a row of trees
that went to the water.
It was a warm afternoon in August
and there was a party
about to begin.
He leaned forward over the paper
and he wrote:

I waited with my cousins across the lake,
watching the grown-ups walking on the far side
along the bank shaded by elms. It was hot.
The sky was clear. My cousins and I stood
for hours among the heavy branches, watching
our parents, and it seemed as if nothing would enter
their lives to make them change, not even the man
running over the lawn, waving a sheet
of paper and shouting. They moved beyond the claims
of weather, beyond whatever news there was,
and did not see the dark begin to deepen
in the trees and bushes, and rise in the folds
of their own dresses and in the stiff white
of their own shirts. Waves of laughter carried
over the water where we, the children, were watching.

It was a scene that was not ours. We were
too far away, and soon we would leave.

He leaned back.
How could he know
the scene was not his?
The summer was with him,
the voices had returned and he saw the faces.
The day had started before the party;
it had rained in the morning
and suddenly cleared in time.
The hems of the dresses were wet.
The men's shoes glistened.
There was a cloud shaped like a hand
which kept lowering.
There was no way to know
why there were times that afternoon
the lawn seemed empty, or why even then
the voices of the grown-ups lingered there.
He took what he had written
and put it aside.
He sat down and began again:

We all went down to the lake, over the lawn,
walking, not saying a word. All the way
from the house, along the shade cast by the elms.
And the sun bore down, lifting the dampness, allowing
the lake to shine like a clear plate surrounded
by mist. We sat and stared at the water and then
lay down on the grass and slept. The air turned colder.
The wind shook the trees. We lay so long we imagined
a hand brushing the fallen leaves from our faces.
But it was not autumn, and some of us, the youngest,

got up and went to the other side of the lake
and stared at the men and women asleep; the men
in stiff white shirts, the women in pale dresses.
We watched all afternoon. And a man ran down
from the house, shouting, waving a sheet of paper.
And the sleepers rose as if nothing had happened,
as if the night had not begun to move
into the trees. We heard their laughter, then
their sighs. They lay back down, and the dark came over
the lawn and covered them. As far as we know
they are still there, their arms crossed over their chests,
their stiff clothing creased. We have never been back.

He looked at what he had written.
How far had he come?
And why had it grown dark just then?
And wasn't he alone when he watched the others
lie down on the lawn?
He stared out the window,
hoping the people at the lake,
the lake itself, would fade.
He wanted to move beyond his past.
He thought of the man
running over the lawn who seemed familiar.
He looked at what he had written
and wondered how he had crossed the lake,
and if his cousins went with him.
Had someone called?
Had someone waved goodbye?
What he had written told him nothing.
He put it away and began again:

I waited under the trees in front of the house,
thinking of nothing, watching the sunlight wash
over the roof. I heard nothing, felt
nothing, even when she appeared in a long
yellow dress, pointed white shoes, her hair
drawn back in a tight bun; even when
she took my hand and led me along the row
of tall trees toward the lake where the rest had gathered,
the men in their starched shirts, the women in
their summer dresses, the children watching the water.
Even then, my life seemed far away
as though it were waiting for me to discover it.
She held my hand and led me toward the water.
The hem of her dress was wet. She said nothing
when she left me with my cousins and joined
the others who stood together. I knew by the way
they talked that something would happen, that some of us,
the youngest, would go away that afternoon
and never find the way back. As I walked through the woods
to the other side of the lake, their voices faded
in the breaking of leaves and branches underfoot.
Though I walked away, I had no sense of going.
I sat and watched the scene across the lake,
I watched and did nothing. Small waves of laughter
carried over the water and then died down.
I was not moved. Even when the man
ran across the lawn, shouting, I did nothing.
It seemed as if the wind drew the dark
from the trees onto the grass. The adults stood
together. They would never leave that shore.
I watched the one in the yellow dress whose name
I had begun to forget and who waited with

the others and who stared at where I was
but could not see me. Already the full moon
had risen and dropped its white ashes on the lake.
And the woman and the others slowly began
to take off their clothes, and the mild rushes of wind
rinsed their skin, their pale bodies shone
briefly among the shadows until they lay
on the damp grass. And the children had all gone.
And that was all. And even then I felt
nothing. I knew that I would never see
the woman in the yellow dress again,
and that the scene by the lake would not be repeated,
and that that summer would be a place too distant
for me ever to find myself in again.
Although I have tried to return, I have always
ended here, where I am now. The lake
still exists, and so does the lawn, though the people
who slept there that afternoon have not been seen since.

It bothered him,
as if too much had been said.
He would have preferred
the lake without a story,
or no story and no lake.
His pursuit was a form of evasion:
the more he tried to uncover
the more there was to conceal
the less he understood.
If he kept it up,
he would lose everything.
He knew this
and remembered what he could—
always at a distance,

on the other side of the lake,
or across the lawn,
always vanishing, always there.
And the woman and the others would save him
and he would save them.
He put his hand on the paper.
He would write a letter for the man
running across the lawn.
He would say what he knew.
He rested his head in his arms and tried to sleep.
He knew that night had once come,
that something had once happened.
He wanted to know but not to know.
Maybe something had happened
one afternoon in August.
Maybe he was there or waiting to be there,
waiting to come running across a lawn
to a lake where people were staring
across the water.
He would come running
and be too late.
The people there would be asleep.
Their children would be watching them.
He would bring what he had written
and then would lie down with the others.
He would be the man
he had become, the man
who would run across the lawn.
He began again:

I sat in the house that looked down on the lake,
the lawn, the woods beside the lawn. I heard
the children near the shore, their voices lifted

where no memory of the place would reach.
I watched the women, the men in white, strolling
in the August heat. I shut the window
and saw them in the quiet glass, passing
each time farther away. The trees began
to darken and the children left. I saw
the distant water fade in the gray shade
of grass and underbrush across the lake.
I thought I saw the children sitting, watching
their parents in a slow parade along
the shore. The shapes among the trees kept changing.
It may have been one child I saw, its face.
It may have been my own face looking back.
I felt myself descend into the future.
I saw beyond the lawn, beyond the lake,
beyond the waiting dark, the end of summer,
the end of autumn, the icy air, the silence,
and then, again, the windowpane. I was
where I was, where I would be, and where I am.
I watched the men and women as the white
eye of the lake began to close and deepen
into blue, then into black. It was too late
for them to call the children. They lay on the grass
and the wind blew and shook the first leaves loose.
I wanted to tell them something. I saw myself
running, waving a sheet of paper, shouting,
telling them all that I had something to give them,
but when I got there, they were gone.

He looked up from the paper
and saw himself in the window.
It was an August night
and he was tired,

and the trees swayed
and the wind shook the window.
It was late.
It did not matter.
He would never catch up
with his past. His life
was slowing down.
It was going.
He could feel it,
could hear it in his speech.
It sounded like nothing,
yet he would pass it on.
And his children would live in it
and they would pass it on,
and it would always sound
like hope dying, like space opening,
like a lawn, or a lake,
or an afternoon.
And pain could not give it
the meaning it lacked;
there was no pain,
only disappearance.
Why had he begun in the first place?
He was tired,
and gave himself up to sleep,
and slept where he was,
and slept without dreaming,
so that when he woke
it seemed as if nothing had happened.
The lake opened like a white eye,
the elms rose over the lawn,
the sun over the elms.
It was as he remembered it—

the mist, the dark, the heat,
the woods on the other side.
He sat for a long time
and saw that they had come
and were on the lawn.
They were waiting for him,
staring up at the window.
The wind blew their hair
and they made no motion.
He was afraid to follow them.
He knew what would happen.
He knew the children would wander off,
that he would lie down with their parents.
And he was afraid.
When they turned
and walked down to the lake
into the shade cast by the elms
the children did wander off.
He saw them in the distance,
across the lake, and wondered if one
would come back someday
and be where he was now.
He saw the adults on the lawn,
beginning to lie down.
And he wanted to warn them,
to tell them what he knew.
He ran from the house down to the lake,
knowing that he would be late,
that he would be left
to continue.
When he got there,
they were gone,
and he was alone in the dark,

unable to speak.
He stood still.
He felt the world recede
into the clouds,
into the shelves of air.
He closed his eyes.
He thought of the lake,
the closets of weeds.
He thought of the moth asleep
in the dust of its wings,
of the bat hanging in the caves of trees.
He felt himself at that moment to be
more than his need to survive,
more than his losses,
because he was less than anything.
He swayed back and forth.
The silence was in him
and it rose like joy,
like the beginning.
When he opened his eyes,
the silence had spread, the sheets
of darkness seemed endless,
the sheets he held in his hand.
He turned and walked to the house.
He went to the room
that looked out on the lawn.
He sat and began to write:

THE UNTELLING

To the Woman in the Yellow Dress

THE
MONUMENT

To the translator of
The Monument
in the future:
"Siste Viator"

I

Let me introduce myself. I am . . . and so on and so forth. Now you know more about me than I know about you.

2

I am setting out from the meeting with what I am, with what I now begin to be, my descendant and my ancestor, my father and my son, my unlike likeness. *

Though I am reaching over hundreds of years as if they did not exist, imagining you at this moment trying to imagine me, and proving finally that imagination accomplishes more than history, you know me better than I know you. Maybe my voice is dim as it reaches over so many years, so many that they seem one long blur erased and joined by events and lives that become one event, one life; even so, my voice is sufficient to make The Monument out of this moment.

---

*Source for this and all quotations in *The Monument* are listed in the Acknowledgments, pp. 161–2.

3

And just as there are areas of our soul which flower and give fruit only beneath the gaze of some spirit come from the eternal region to which they belong in time, just so, when that gaze is hidden from us by absence, these areas long for that magical gaze like the earth longing for the sun so that it may give out flowering plants and fruit.

> *Shine alone, shine nakedly, shine like bronze,*
> *that reflects neither my face nor any inner part*
> *of my being, shine like fire, that mirrors nothing.*

Why have I chosen this way to continue myself under your continuing gaze? I might have had my likeness carved in stone, but it is not my image that I want you to have, nor my life, nor the life around me, only this document. What I include of myself is unreal and distracting. Only this luminous moment has life, this instant in which we both write, this flash of voice.

4

Look in thy glass, and tell the face thou viewest
Now is the time that face should form another . . .

Many would have thought it an Happiness to have had
their lot of Life in some notable Conjunctures of Ages
past; but the uncertainty of future Times hath tempted
few to make a part in Ages to come.

And the secret of human life, the universal secret, the
root secret from which all other secrets spring, is the
longing for more life, the furious and insatiable desire
to be everything else without ever ceasing to be our-
selves, to take possession of the entire universe without
letting the universe take possession of us and absorb
us; it is the desire to be someone else without ceasing to
be myself, and continue being myself at the same time I
am someone else. . . .

It is a struggle to believe I am writing to someone else,
to you, when I imagine the spectral conditions of your
existence. This work has allowed you to exist, yet this
work exists because you are translating it. Am I wrong?
It must be early morning as you write. You sit in a large,
barely furnished room with one window from which
you can see a gray body of water on which several
black ducks are asleep. How still the world is so many
years from now. How few people there are. They never
leave town, never visit the ruins of the great city.

5

Or let me put it this way. You must imagine that you are the author of this work, that the wind is blowing from the northeast, bringing rain that slaps and spatters against your windows. You must imagine the ocean's swash and backwash sounding hushed and muffled. Imagine a long room with a light at one end, illuminating a desk, a chair, papers. Imagine someone is in the chair. Imagine he is you; it is long ago and you are dressed in the absurd clothes of the time. You must imagine yourself asking the question: which of us has sought the other?

6

I have no rest from myself. I feel as though I am devouring my whole life. . . .

O my soul, I gave you all, and I have emptied all my hands to you; and now—now you say to me, smiling and full of melancholy, "Which of us has to be thankful? Should not the giver be thankful that the receiver received? Is not giving a need? Is not receiving a mercy?"

All voice is but echo caught from a soundless voice.

In what language do I live? I live in none. I live in you. It is your voice that I begin to hear and it has no language. I hear the motions of a spirit and the sound of what is secret becomes, for me, a voice that is your voice speaking in my ear. It is a misery unheard of to know the secret has no name, no language I can learn.

7

O if you knew! If you knew! How it has been. How the ladies of the house would talk softly in the moonlight under the orange trees of the courtyard, impressing upon me the sweetness of their voices and something mysterious in the quietude of their lives. O the heaviness of that air, the perfume of jasmine, pale lights against the stones of the courtyard walls. Monument! Monument! How will you ever know!

Then do thy office, Muse; I teach thee how
To make him seem, long hence, as he shows now.

Through you I shall be born again; myself again and
again; myself without others; myself with a tomb;
myself beyond death. I imagine you taking my name; I
imagine you saying "myself myself" again and again.
And suddenly there will be no blue sky or sun or shape
of anything without that simple utterance.

9

. . . Nothing must stand

Between you and the shapes you take
When the crust of shape has been destroyed.

You as you are? You are yourself.

It has been necessary to submit to vacancy in order to begin again, to clear ground, to make space. I can allow nothing to be received. Therein lies my triumph *and* my mediocrity. Nothing is the destiny of everyone, it is our commonness made dumb. I am passing it on. The Monument is a void, artless and everlasting. What I was I am no longer. I speak for nothing, the nothing that I am, the nothing that is this work. And you shall perpetuate me not in the name of what I was, but in the name of what I am.

10

Perhaps there is no monument and this is invisible writing that has appeared in fate's corridor; you are no mere translator but an interpreter-angel.

II

I begin to sense your impatience. It is hard for you to believe that I am what you were. It is a barren past that I represent—one that would have you be its sole guardian. But consider how often we are given to invent ourselves; maybe once, but even so we say we are another, another entirely similar.

Stories are told of people who die and after a moment come back to life, telling of a radiance and deep calm they experienced. I too died once but said nothing until this moment, not wishing to upset my friends or to allow my enemies jokes about whether I was really alive to begin with. It happened a couple of years ago in March or April. I was having coffee. I know I was dead just a few minutes because the coffee was still warm when I came back. I saw no light, felt no radiance. I saw my life flash before me as a succession of meals and I felt full. This feeling was to give way to an image of waste. How much would be lost! A box placed underground with me inside would never be right. And then I thought of The Monument. It was this promise of adequate memorial that brought me back to life, to my room and my coffee.

Stars denote places where The Monument has been reported.

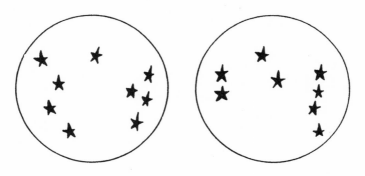

Eastern Hemisphere   *Western Hemisphere*

14

It may be wise at this time to get down to practical matters, to make suggestions that will ease your task. There are words that I use, words used often in the poetry of my day, which should not constrain you. It is possible that they will not exist in your time or in your language. In either case, find words for which you yourself have a fondness. If this is difficult, then I suggest you use one word to cover the many. The objects you see from where you sit may be "anything." "Anything" may be "nothing," depending on what your feeling is. If "nothing" conveys the wrong idea, use "something." By all means, use "something" if you agree with the poet who shrieks, "There is not nothing, no, no, never nothing."

15

The certainty of death is attended by uncertainties, in time, manner, places. The variety of Monuments hath often obscured true graves: and Cenotaphs confounded Sepulchres.

The true Monument must survive, must stand by itself despite the possible survival of false monuments. Do not be taken in by structures that call themselves The Monument and look like this:

THE MONUMENT

During the night
a storm broke,
striking the monument,
sending it down,
stone and green
pieces of bronze,
onto the lawn.
Now it lies
among shrubs
and torn limbs
of trees.   You scrape
the pieces clean,
cracks and channels
made by rain, you scrub
away the scars, stains,
names painted
on the pedestal.

When you are done,
nothing about
the monument
will look the same.
The cape will gleam,
curls of hair
will seem to swirl
in the moonlight
or spill
in the bright sun.
No wind will scream
under the arms or chin;
all signs and syllables
of pain will be
rephrased, and when
you leave the monument's
hard gaze, the cold
violet of its shade,
you will not think
of turning back.
Not even fears
of slow decay,
of fires blazing
at its base
will keep you there.
Before you walk away,
you will drop a list
inside its throat
of what to do in case
it falls again.
Your final say
buried in the monument's
cold shape . . .

16

Or look like this:

THE MONUMENT

You will see it
in the shade or covered
with a shawl
of sunlight or sheen
of wet gray;
or later, barely
visible while
the night passes
with its silent cargo
of moons and stars.
You will see sleeping
figures at its feet;
you will see
in its bleached eyes
baked by sun,
strafed by rain,
the meanness of
the sky; and in
its barely open mouth
perpetual twilight.
You will see it
when you come
and when you leave,
you will see it
when you do not wish to

and you will never know
whose monument it is
or why it came to you . . .

17

How sad it is to come back to one's work, so much less than the world it masks or echoes or reminds one of. Such dreariness to return to one's singleness, one's simple reductions. Poems have come to seem so little. Even The Monument is little. How it wishes it were something it cannot be—its own perpetual birth instead of its death again and again, each sentence a memorial.

18

If you want me again look for me under your boot-soles.

> *Who walks where I am not,*
> *Who remains standing when I die.*

The Unmonument is my memorial placed upside down in the earth. This least obtrusive of reminders will disturb no one, being in fact a way of burying my death. The inverse of such a tactic would be the unburial of my life. That is, so long as my monument is underground, my life shall remain above. Friend, you are my collaborator in this venture. How much pleasure it gives me to imagine you standing on the very ground that covers my statue, saying:

> *From south and east and west and north,*
> *roads coming together have led me*
> *to my secret center . . .*

And of course it will be late in the day and you will consider the events of your life from the greatest to the most humble. Again words will come to you:

> *Now I can forget them. I reach my center . . .*
> *my mirror.*
> *Soon I shall know who I am.*

Spare my bones the fire,
Let me lie entire,
Underground or in the air,
Whichever, I don't care.

Remember the story of my death? Well, I planned it this far in advance. And I did it for you, so you might understand it as none of the others could. When I leaned back on the cold pillows, staring through the open window at the black velvety sky, pointing, though my hand was on the verge of collapsing, and said in a clear, calm voice, "Look! Look!", I was asking the impossible of those loyal friends who were crowded into that small room. For they looked out the window and, seeing nothing, said almost in unison, "What is it?" And I replied in a tone that soothed and urged at once, "There! There!" In a moment I was dead. That is the famous story of my death told, I believe, for a dozen or so years and then forgotten. It is yours because you have found The Monument. Finding The Monument is what I urged when I said, "Look! Look!"

It is my belief that on a certain day in a person's life the shapes of all the clouds in the sky will for a single moment directly over his head resemble him. It has been the sad lot of almost everyone who has ever lived to miss this spectacle, but it has not been so with me. Today I saw The Monument affirmed in heaven. I sat in a chair and looked up by chance and this is what I saw.

A story is told of a man who lived his life anticipating his moment in the heavens, and each day there were clouds he would lie on his back in front of his house. He did this summer and winter and the only rest he got was on clear days or days completely overcast. Finally, when he was very old, he did see himself in the clouds and died immediately after. They found him up on his platform, his eyes wide open, the look of astonishment still upon them.

We are truly ourselves only when we coincide with nothing, not even ourselves.

Where do I come from? Though unimportant and irrelevant to so single-minded a venture as The Monument, I believe if I included a few paragraphs from an abandoned autobiography you would see for yourself that I am justified in leaving my life out of our work.

I have always said, when speaking of my father's father, Emil, that he died a sudden and tragic death by falling into a giant vat of molten metal. The fact is I know only what my father told me—that he suffered an accident in a steel mill and died. The terseness of my father's explanation (no doubt masking some pain at recalling this stage in his own life) created an impression of mystery and violence in my mind. Since the vat of molten metal was the only image I had of the inside of a steel mill, it actually became for me the sole cause of my grandfather's death. And the horror of it put him in a heroic perspective, a perspective which contributed to my impulse to aggrandize my father. As a small boy I wanted a lineage of heroes. It is significant that I would usually add, as epilogue to the tale of Emil's death, the suggestion that he was now part of a Cleveland skyscraper. There is some primitive irony in this, but also a belief in the ultimate utility of his dying, as though it were not merely an accident but self-sacrifice for the public good. His death has become over the years a myth of origin to which I cling almost unconsciously. I say "almost" because whenever I tell of it I am aware of the slight distortion I may be guilty of. Nevertheless, I feel a compulsion to tell it the way I originally construed it, regardless of the doubts that have increased over the years, and the young boy in me is satisfied.

Of my father's mother, Ida, I have no image whatever, probably because my father had none either. She died giving birth to him. He weighed fifteen pounds.

. . . he ordered them to dig a grave at once, of the right size, and then collect any pieces of marble that they could find and fetch wood and water for the disposal of the corpse. As they bustled about obediently he muttered through his tears: "Dead! And so great an artist!"

It is good none of my enemies, friends, or colleagues has seen this, for they would complain of my narcissism as they always seem to, but with—so they would claim—greater cause. They would mistake this modest document as self-centered in the extreme, not only because none of their names appears in it, but because I have omitted to mention my wife or daughter. How mistaken they are. This poor document does not have to do with a self, it dwells on the absence of a self. I— and this pronoun will have to do—have not permitted anything worthwhile or memorable to be part of this communication that strains even to exist in a language other than the one in which it was written. So much is excluded that it could not be a document of self-centeredness. If it is a mirror to anything, it is to the gap between the nothing that was and the nothing that will be. It is a thread of longing that binds past and future. Again, it is everything that history is not.

—— 23

It is easy to lose oneself in nothing because nothing can interrupt and be unnoticed. Why do I do this?

24

There is a day when the daughters of Necessity sit on their thrones and chant and souls gather to choose the next life they will live. After the despots pick beggary, and the beggars pick wealth, and Orpheus picks swan-hood, Agamemnon an eagle, Ajax a lion, and Odysseus the life of quiet obscurity, I come along, pushing my way through the musical animals, and pick one of the lots. Since I had no need to compensate for any previous experience and wandered onto that meadow by chance, I found the lot of another man much like me, which is how I found you. And instead of going to the River of Unmindfulness, I wrote this down.

The most enclosed being generates waves.

Suppose the worst happens and I am still around while you are reading this? Suppose everybody is around? Well, there is the crystal box!

26

I confess a yearning to make prophetic remarks, to be remembered as someone who was ahead of his time; I would like to be someone about whom future generations would say, as they shifted from foot to foot and stared at the ground, "He knew! He knew!" But I don't know. I know only you, you ahead of my time. I know it is sad, even silly, this longing to say something that will charm or amaze others later on. But one little phrase is all I ask. Friend, say something amazing *for* me. It must be something you take for granted, something meaningless to you, but impossible for me to think of. Say I predicted it. Write it here:

[Translator's note: *Though I wanted to obey the author's request, I could not without violating what I took to be his desire for honesty. I believe he not only wanted it this way, but might have predicted it.*]

I am so glad you discovered me. The treatment I have received is appalling. The army of angry poets coming out to whip The Monument.

28

I have begun to mistrust you, my dear friend, and I am sorry. As I proceed with this work, I sense your wish to make it your own. True, I have, in a way, given it to you but it is precisely this spirit of "giving" that must be preserved. You must not "take" what is not really yours. No doubt I am being silly, my fears reflecting jealousy on my part, but I know you only as you work on this text. Whatever else you are is hidden from me. What I fear is that you will tell people in your day that you made up The Monument, that this is a mock translation, that I am merely a creature of your imagination. I know that I intend this somewhat, but the sweet anonymity and nothingness that I claim as my province *do* cause me pain. As I write I feel that this should not be my memorial, merely, but that it should be passed on in no one's name, not even yours.

29

It occurs to me that you may be a woman. What then? I suppose I become therefore a woman. If you are a woman, I suggest that you curl up inside the belly of The Monument which is buried horizontally in the ground and eventually let yourself out through the mouth. Thus, I can experience, however belatedly, a birth, your birth, the birth of myself as a woman.

. . . a Poet's mind
Is labour not unworthy of regard.

And what I say unto you, I say unto all, Watch!

Sometimes when I wander in these woods whose prince I am, I hear a voice and I know that I am not alone. Another voice, another monument becoming one; another tomb, another marker made from elements least visible; another voice that says *Watch it closely*. And I do, and there is someone inside. It is the Bishop, who after all was not intended to be seen. It is the Bishop calling and calling.

Such good work as yours should not go unrewarded, so I have written a speech for you, knowing how tired you must be. It should be delivered into the mirror.

Labors of hate! Labors of love! I can't go on working this way, shedding darkness, shucking light, peeling pages. There is no virtue in it. The author is the opposite of a good author, allowing no people in his work, allowing no plot to carry it forward. Where are the good phrases? They're borrowed! It all adds up to greed—his words in my mouth, his time in my time. He longs to be alive, to continue, yet he says he is nobody. Does he have nothing to say? Probably not. Anonymous, his eyes are fixed upon himself. I grow tired of his jabbering, the freight of his words. My greatest hope is his continued anonymity, which is why I bother to finish The Monument.

[Translator's note: *I must say that he has expressed my feeling so adequately that I find myself admiring him for it and hating myself somewhat.*]

32

Flotillas! Floating gardens skimming the sky's blue shell. Great gangs of gang-gangs and galahs. The air has never been so pure, my lungs are two pink sacks of moist down-under light. Friend, The Monument shines in the tabernacle of air, and at night, under the Southern Cross and the silent sparkling bed of stars, it sings. Friend, this is the place to do your monument. Go among the gang-gangs and galahs!

33

The drift of skeletons under the earth, the shifting of that dark society, those nations of the dead, the unshaping of their bones into dirt, the night of nothing removing them, turning their absences into the small zeros of the stars, it is indeed a grave, invisible workmanship. O Monument, what can be done!

34

They are back, the angry poets. But look! They have come with hammers and little buckets, and they are knocking off pieces of The Monument to study and use in the making of their own small tombs.

35

SONG OF MYSELF

First silence, then some humming,
then more silence, then nothing,
then more nothing, then silence,
then more silence, then nothing.

Song of My Other Self: There is no other self.

The Wind's Song: Get out of my way.

The Sky's Song: You're less than a cloud.

The Tree's Song: You're less than a leaf.

The Sea's Song: You're a wave, less than a wave.

The Sun's Song: You're the moon's child.

The Moon's Song: You're no child of mine.

36

There is a sullen, golden greed in my denials. Yet I wish I were not merely making them up; I wish I could be the lies I tell. This is the truth. Knowledge never helped me sort out anything, and having had no knowledge but of nothing suggests all questions are unanswerable once they are posed. Asking is the act of unresolving, a trope for disclosure.

. . . it is to be remembered, that to raise a Monument is a sober and reflective act; that the inscription which it bears is intended to be permanent and for universal perusal; and that, for this reason, the thoughts and feelings expressed should be permanent also—liberated from that weakness and anguish of sorrow which is in nature transitory, and which with instinctive decency retires from notice. The passions should be subdued, the emotions controlled; strong indeed, but nothing ungovernable or wholly involuntary. Seemliness requires this, and truth requires it also: for how can the Narrator otherwise be trusted?

Julius Scaliger, who in a sleepless Fit of the Gout could make two hundred Verses in a Night, would have but five plain Words upon his Tomb.

Tell me that my ugly tomb, my transcending gesture, my way into the next world, your world, my world made by you, you the future of me, my future, my features translated, tell me that it will improve, that it will seem better for my not giving in to what passes for style, that its prose shall never wear a poem's guise at last, tell me that its perpetual prose will become less than itself and hint always at more.

38

The epic of disbelief
blares oftener and soon . . .

Some will think I wrote this and some will think you
wrote this. The fact is neither of us did. There is a
ghostly third who has taken up residence in this pen,
this pen we hold. Not tangible enough to be described
but easy to put a finger on, it is the text already writ-
ten, unwriting itself into the text of promise. It blooms
in its ashes, radiates health in its sickness. It is a new
falsity, electric in its clumsiness, glad in its lies. And it
loves itself as it fears death.

39

I wonder if my poverty would be more complete without you or whether you complete it, the last straw taken away. Having said such a thing I feel a surge of power, I, a single strand, upright, making translation less and less possible. Beautiful swipes of clarity fall upon me, lights from the luminous bells of heaven. I tell you this robe of harmless flames I wear is no poor man's torn pajamas. There's no poverty here, with or without you. Translate. Translate faster. Brief work, isn't it, this feathery fluke!

To be the first of the posthumous poets is to be the oldest. This will make children of the poets of Europe, the dead poets of Europe. There must be something America is first in. Death and post-death meditations! Glory be! A crown on our heads at last! But what is America to you or you to America?

Solemn truths! Lucid inescapable foolishness! None of that for me! To be the salt of Walt, oceanic in osteality! Secure in cenotaph! The hysterical herald of hypogea! The fruit of the tomb! The flute of the tomb! The loot of gloom! The lute of loot! The work of soon, of never and ever! Saver of naught. Naughtiness of severance. Hoot of hiddenness. I give you my graven grave, my wordy ossuary, tell-tale trinket of transcendence, bauble of babble, tower of tripe, trap of tribute, thought-taxi from one day to the next, nougat of nothing, germ of gemini, humble hypogeum!

42

We have come to terms without terms, come round almost to the end. A relief, but only a stage, bare stage, first stage. We have allowed the enormous airs of the future to engulf us—to be sung, to be borne and born. Heirs of ourselves, ourselves heirs, salvos of air. Without weight the future is possible, here without our waiting. I embrace you in this madness, this muscular mouthing of possibles. The enormous airs—the giant cloudsongs that will reign and reign. Friend, they are coming and only we know it. Perhaps we should be silent, tell no one and the airs will pass, pass without knowledge of themselves, never having been termed, tuned in turmoil, termed harmless.

43

Heavy glory upon us. Hang on. I must praise my brothers and sisters in the lost art, spitting into the wind, beating their heads against the stars, eating their words, putting their feet in their mouths, hating each other, all of them either lovely or fearful.

44

I feel nostalgia for poetry and believe The Monument should have some lines like:

> Invisible lords among the stars
> Over the heads of deep astronomers

or:

> The moon sucking the sea, sucking
> The light from our eyes as we sleep

That sort of thing. But it would never do. Too hard to translate out of the original. After the blazing plainness of The Monument's prose it doesn't stand up. And yet, there's a longing that has no voice and wants one, that fears it will die of itself. There are moments that crave memorial as if they were worthy, as if they were history and not merely in it, moments of the bluest sky, of the most intense sun, of the greatest happiness of the least known man or woman, moments that may have gone on for years in the most remote village on earth. They shall exist outside The Monument.

45

We are the enemies of pastoral violence, lovers of cold; the body recumbent like The Monument is for us the goodest good; heavy allusions to weather are just another load to us. Give us a good cigar, a long ash that we can speculate on. And plenty of smoke. Ho hum. Now give us a glass of Spanish brandy. Give us a blank wall that we might see ourselves more truly and more strange. Now give us the paper, the daily paper on which to write. Now give us the day, this day. Take it away. The space that is left is The Monument.

46

It is the crystal box again. Let it be a sunlit tomb, a clear tumulus. Let us stand by it, by the life it promises. If we bask in its brightness, we shall be saved, we shall grow into the language that calls from the future, The Monument reaching out.

47

*Spin out from your entrails, therefore, my soul, and let
come what may! More empty space, more void . . .*

> *Till the bridge you will need be form'd, till the
> ductile anchor hold,*
> *Till the gossamer thread you fling catch some-
> where, O my soul.*

Prose is the language of meaning so I suppose I mean
what I say. I say what I say because it is prose. And so
it is; describing the circle, the naught of my means, I
am taking away, subtracting myself from my words.
My blank prose travels into the future, its freight the
fullness of zero, the circumference of absence. And it
misses something, something I remember I wanted.
Soon I shall disappear into the well of want, the *lux* of
lack.

48

It is the giant of nothingness that rises beyond, that rises beyond beyondness, undiscovered in the vault of the future, in the leap of faith. If there were a limb here, a limb there, on the desert sand, *that* would be something. If on the pedestal these words appeared: "I am The Monument. Should you doubt this, look around you and compare," *that* would be something. But The Monument has no monument. There are no powers that will work for it; earth, sky, and breathing of the common air, all will forget. O most unhappy Monument! The giant of nothingness rising in sleep like the beginning of language, like language being born into the sleeper's future, his dream of himself entering the beyond. O happy Monument! The giant of nothing is taking you with him!

49

I have no apologies, no words for disbelievers. What do I care if there is nothing sublime in this summery encounter with the void or voided mirror? We go our ways, each without the other, going without a theory of direction, going because we have to. Why make excuses? Friend, tell them I see myself only as happy. Let them say what they will, The Monument will pretend to be dead.

50

Here I lie dead, and here I wait for thee:
So thou shalt wait
Soon for some other; since all mortals be
Bound to one fate.

Our Fathers finde their graves in our short memories,
and sadly tell us how we may be buried in our Sur-
vivors.

Now here I am at the end waiting for you, ahead of my
time, ahead of yours. Such irony should be its own
reward, but here I am at the end, the letter ended, The
Monument concluded, but only briefly; for it must
continue, must gather its words and send them off into
another future, your future, my future. O poor Monu-
ment to offer so little even to those who have made
you!

51

If I were to die now without The Monument, none of my words would remain. How sad it is to think of the hours wasted while this triumph of ease and crudity that has taken so little time should last centuries, towering over the corpses of poems whose lyrical natures flew off like the best intentions. If I were to die now, I would change my name so it might appear that the author of my works were still alive. No I wouldn't. If I were to die now, it would be only a joke, a cruel joke played on fortune. If I were to die now, your greatest work would remain forever undone. My last words would be, "Don't finish it."

—— 52

. . . Oh, how do I bear to go on living! And how could I bear to die now!

> *O living always, always dying!*
> *O the burials of me past and present,*
> *O me while I stride ahead, material, visible, imperi-*
>   *ous as ever;*
> *O me, what I was for years, now dead, (I lament*
>   *not, I am content;)*
> *O to disengage myself from those corpses of me,*
>   *which I turn and look at where I cast them,*
> *To pass on, (O living! always living!) and leave the*
>   *corpses behind.*

THE LATE
HOUR

I

Another Place

THE COMING OF LIGHT

Even this late it happens:
the coming of love, the coming of light.
You wake and the candles are lit as if by themselves,
stars gather, dreams pour into your pillows,
sending up warm bouquets of air.
Even this late the bones of the body shine
and tomorrow's dust flares into breath.

ANOTHER PLACE

I walk
into what light
there is

not enough for blindness
or clear sight
of what is to come

yet I see
the water
the single boat
the man standing

he is not someone I know

this is another place
what light there is
spreads like a net
over nothing

what is to come
has come to this
before

this is the mirror
in which pain is asleep
this is the country
nobody visits

LINES FOR WINTER

for Ros Krauss

Tell yourself
as it gets cold and gray falls from the air
that you will go on
walking, hearing
the same tune no matter where
you find yourself—
inside the dome of dark
or under the cracking white
of the moon's gaze in a valley of snow.
Tonight as it gets cold
tell yourself
what you know which is nothing
but the tune your bones play
as you keep going. And you will be able
for once to lie down under the small fire
of winter stars.
And if it happens that you cannot
go on or turn back
and you find yourself
where you will be at the end,
tell yourself
in that final flowing of cold through your limbs
that you love what you are.

MY SON

(after Carlos Drummond de Andrade)

My son,
my only son,
the one I never had,
would be a man today.

He moves
in the wind,
fleshless, nameless.
Sometimes

he comes
and leans his head,
lighter than air
against my shoulder

and I ask him,
Son,
where do you stay,
where do you hide?

And he answers me
with a cold breath,
You never noticed
though I called

and called
and keep on calling
from a place
beyond,

beyond love,
where nothing,
everything,
wants to be born.

WHITE

for Harold Bloom

Now in the middle of my life
all things are white.
I walk under the trees,
the frayed leaves,
the wide net of noon,
and the day is white.
And my breath is white,
drifting over the patches
of grass and fields of ice
into the high circles of light.
As I walk, the darkness of
my steps is also white,
and my shadow blazes
under me. In all seasons
the silence where I find myself
and what I make of nothing are white,
the white of sorrow,
the white of death.
Even the night that calls
like a dark wish is white;
and in my sleep as I turn
in the weather of dreams
it is the white of my sheets
and white shades of the moon
drawn over my floor
that save me for morning.
And out of my waking
the circle of light widens,
it fills with trees, houses,
stretches of ice.

It reaches out. It rings
the eye with white.
All things are one.
All things are joined
even beyond the edge of sight.

FOR JESSICA, MY DAUGHTER

Tonight I walked,
lost in my own meditation,
and was afraid,
not of the labyrinth
that I have made of love and self
but of the dark and faraway.
I walked, hearing the wind in the trees,
feeling the cold against my skin,
but what I dwelled on
were the stars blazing
in the immense arc of sky.

Jessica, it is so much easier
to think of our lives,
as we move under the brief luster of leaves,
loving what we have,
than to think of how it is
such small beings as we
travel in the dark
with no visible way
or end in sight.

Yet there were times I remember
under the same sky
when the body's bones became light
and the wound of the skull
opened to receive
the cold rays of the cosmos,
and were, for an instant,
themselves the cosmos,

there were times when I could believe
we were the children of stars
and our words were made of the same
dust that flames in space,
times when I could feel in the lightness of breath
the weight of a whole day
come to rest.

But tonight
it is different.
Afraid of the dark
in which we drift or vanish altogether,
I imagine a light
that would not let us stray too far apart,
a secret moon or mirror,
a sheet of paper,
something you could carry
in the dark
when I am away.

II

From the Long Sad Party

FROM THE LONG SAD PARTY

Someone was saying
something about shadows covering the field, about
how things pass, how one sleeps towards morning
and the morning goes.

Someone was saying
how the wind dies down but comes back,
how shells are the coffins of wind
but the weather continues.

It was a long night
and someone said something about the moon shedding its white
on the cold field, that there was nothing ahead
but more of the same.

Someone mentioned
a city she had been in before the war, a room with two candles
against a wall, someone dancing, someone watching.
We began to believe

the night would not end.
Someone was saying the music was over and no one had noticed.
Then someone said something about the planets, about the stars,
how small they were, how far away.

THE LATE HOUR

A man walks towards town,
a slack breeze smelling of earth
and the raw green of trees blows at his back.

He drags the weight of his passion as if nothing were over,
as if the woman, now curled in bed beside her lover,
still cared for him.

She is awake and stares at scars of light
trapped in the panes of glass.
He stands under her window, calling her name;

he calls all night and it makes no difference.
It will happen again, he will come back wherever she is.
Again he will stand outside and imagine

her eyes opening in the dark
and see her rise to the window and peer down.
Again she will lie awake beside her lover

and hear the voice from somewhere in the dark.
Again the late hour, the moon and stars,
the wounds of night that heal without sound,

again the luminous wind of morning that comes before the sun.
And, finally, without warning or desire,
the lonely and the feckless end.

SEVEN DAYS

First Day

I sat in a room that was almost dark,
looking out to sea. There was a light on the water
that released a rainbow which landed near the stairs.
I was surprised to discover you at the end of it.

Second Day

I sat in a beach chair surrounded by tall grass
so that only the top of my hat showed.
The sky kept shifting but the sunlight stayed.
It was a glass pillar filled with bright dust, and you were inside.

Third Day

A comet with two tails appeared. You were between them
with your arms outspread as if you were keeping the tails apart.
I wished you would speak but you didn't. I knew then
that you might remain silent forever.

Fourth Day

This evening in my room there was a pool of pink light
that floated on the wooden floor and I thought of the night
you sailed away. I closed my eyes and tried to think
of ways we might be reconciled; I could not think of one.

Fifth Day

A light appeared and I thought the dawn had come.
But the light was in the mirror and became brighter
the closer I moved. You were staring at me.
I watched you until morning but you never spoke.

Sixth Day

It was in the afternoon but I was sure
there was moonlight trapped under the plates.
You were standing outside the window, saying, "Lift them up."
When I lifted them up the sea was dark,
the wind was from the west, and you were gone.

Seventh Day

I went for a walk late at night wondering whether
you would come back. The air was warm and the odor of roses
made me think of the day you appeared in my room,
in a pool of light. Soon the moon would rise
and I hoped you would come. In the meantime I thought
of the old stars falling and the ashes of one thing and another.
I knew that I would be scattered among them,
that the dream of light would continue without me,
for it was never my dream, it was yours. And it was clear
in the dark of the seventh night that my time would come soon.
I looked at the hill, I looked out over the calm water.
Already the moon was rising and you were here.

ABOUT A MAN

Would get up at night,
go to the mirror and ask:
Who's here?

Would turn, sink to his knees
and stare at snow falling blameless
in the night air.

Would cry:
Heaven, look down!
See? No one is here.

Would take off his clothes and say:
My flesh is a grave with nothing inside.

Would lean to the mirror:
You there, you, wake me,
tell me none of what I've said is true.

THE STORY

It is the old story: complaints about the moon
sinking into the sea, about stars in the first light fading,
about the lawn wet with dew, the lawn silver, the lawn cold.

It goes on and on: a man stares at his shadow
and says it's the ash of himself falling away, says his days
are the real black holes in space. But none of it's true.

You know the one I mean: it's the one about the minutes dying,
and the hours, and the years; it's the story I tell
about myself, about you, about everyone.

FOR HER

Let it be anywhere
on any night you wish,
in your room that is empty and dark

or down the street
or at those dim frontiers
you barely see, barely dream of.

You will not feel desire,
nothing will warn you,
no sudden wind, no stillness of air.

She will appear,
looking like someone you knew:
the friend who wasted her life,

the girl who sat under the palm tree.
Her bracelets will glitter,
becoming the lights

of a village you turned from years ago.

SO YOU SAY

It is all in the mind, you say, and has
nothing to do with happiness. The coming of cold,
the coming of heat, the mind has all the time in the world.
I wish the bottom of things were not so far away.

You take my arm and say something will happen,
something unusual for which we were always prepared,
like the sun arriving after a day in Asia,
like the moon departing after a night with us.

POEMS OF AIR

The poems of air are slowly dying;
too light for the page, too faint, too far away,
the ones we've called The Moon, The Stars, The Sun,
sink into the sea or slide behind the cooling trees
at the field's edge. The grave of light is everywhere.

Some summer day or winter night the poems will cease.
No one will weep, no one will look at the sky.
A heavy mist will fill the valleys,
an indelible dark will rain on the hills,
and nothing, not a single bird, will sing.

AN OLD MAN AWAKE IN HIS OWN DEATH

This is the place that was promised
when I went to sleep,
taken from me when I woke.

This is the place unknown to anyone,
where names of ships and stars
drift out of reach.

The mountains are not mountains anymore;
the sun is not the sun.
One tends to forget how it was;

I see myself, I see
the shine of darkness on my brow.
Once I was whole, once I was young . . .

As if it mattered now
and you could hear me
and the weather of this place would ever cease.

NO PARTICULAR DAY

Items of no
particular day
swarm down—

moves of the mind
that never quite
make it as poems:

like the way
you take me aside
and leave me

by the water
with its waves
knitted

like your sweater
like your brow;
moves of the mind

that take us
somewhere near
and leave us

combing the air
for signs
of change,

signs the sky
will break
and shower down

upon us
particular
ideas of light.

EXILES

Only they had escaped
to tell us how
the house had gone
and things had vanished,
how they lay in their beds
and were wakened by the wind
and saw the roof gone
and thought they were dreaming.
But the starry night
and the chill they felt were real.
And they looked around
and saw trees instead of walls.
When the sun rose
they saw nothing of their own.
Other houses were collapsing.
Other trees were falling.
They ran for the train
but the train had gone.
They ran to the river
but there were no boats.
They thought about us.
They would come here.
So they got to their feet
and started to run.
There were no birds.
The wind had died.
Their clothes were tattered

and fell to the ground.
So they ran
and covered themselves
with their hands
and shut their eyes
and imagined us
taking them in.
They could not hear
the sound of their footsteps.
They felt they were drifting.
All day they had run
and now could see nothing,
not even their hands.
Everything faded
around their voices
until only their voices were left,
telling the story.
And after the story,
their voices were gone.

2

They were not gone
and the story they told
was barely begun,
for when the air was silent
and everything faded
it meant only that these
exiles came
into a country
not their own,
into a radiance
without hope.

Having come too far,
they were frightened back
into the night of their origin.
And on their way back
they heard the footsteps
and felt the warmth
of the clothes they thought
had been lifted from them.
They ran by the boats at anchor,
hulking in the bay,
by the train waiting
under the melting frost of stars.
Their sighs were mixed
with the sighs of the wind.
And when the moon rose,
they were still going back.
And when the trees
and houses reappeared,
they saw what they wanted:
the return of their story
to where it began.
They saw it in the cold
room under the roof
chilled by moonlight.
They lay in their beds
and the shadows of the giant trees
brushed darkly against the walls.

III

Poor North

POOR NORTH

It is cold, the snow is deep,
the wind beats around in its cage of trees,
clouds have the look of rags torn and soiled with use,
and starlings peck at the ice.
It is north, poor north. Nothing goes right.

The man of the house has gone to work,
selling chairs and sofas in a failing store.
His wife stays home and stares from the window into the trees,
trying to recall the life she lost, though it wasn't much.
White flowers of frost build up on the glass.

It is late in the day. Brants and Canada geese are asleep
on the waters of St. Margaret's Bay.
The man and his wife are out for a walk; see how they lean
into the wind; they turn up their collars
and the small puffs of their breath are carried away.

WHERE ARE THE WATERS OF CHILDHOOD?

See where the windows are boarded up,
where the gray siding shines in the sun and salt air
and the asphalt shingles on the roof have peeled or fallen off,
where tiers of oxeye daisies float on a sea of grass?
That's the place to begin.

Enter the kingdom of rot,
smell the damp plaster, step over the shattered glass,
the pockets of dust, the rags, the soiled remains of a mattress,
look at the rusted stove and sink, at the rectangular stain
on the wall where Winslow Homer's *Gulf Stream* hung.

Go to the room where your father and mother
would let themselves go in the drift and pitch of love,
and hear, if you can, the creak of their bed,
then go to the place where you hid.

Go to your room, to all the rooms whose cold, damp air you breathed,
to all the unwanted places where summer, fall, winter, spring,
seem the same unwanted season, where the trees you knew have died
and other trees have risen. Visit that other place
you barely recall, that other house half hidden.

See the two dogs burst into sight. When you leave,
they will cease, snuffed out in the glare of an earlier light.
Visit the neighbors down the block; he waters his lawn,
she sits on her porch, but not for long.
When you look again they are gone.

Keep going back, back to the field, flat and sealed in mist,
green the color of light sinking in ice. On the other side,
a man and a woman are waiting; they have come back,
your mother before she was gray, your father before he was white.

Now look at the North West Arm, how it glows a deep cerulean blue.
See the light on the grass, the one leaf burning, the cloud
that flares. You're almost there, in a moment your parents
will disappear, leaving you under the light of a vanished star,
under the dark of a star newly born. Now is the time.

Now you invent the boat of your flesh and set it upon the waters
and drift in the gradual swell, in the laboring salt.
Now you look down. The waters of childhood are there.

POT ROAST

I gaze upon the roast,
that is sliced and laid out
on my plate
and over it
I spoon the juices
of carrot and onion.
And for once I do not regret
the passage of time.

I sit by a window
that looks
on the soot-stained brick of buildings
and do not care that I see
no living thing—not a bird,
not a branch in bloom,
not a soul moving
in the rooms
behind the dark panes.
These days when there is little
to love or to praise
one could do worse
than yield
to the power of food.
So I bend

to inhale
the steam that rises
from my plate, and I think
of the first time
I tasted a roast

like this.
It was years ago
in Seabright,
Nova Scotia;
my mother leaned
over my dish and filled it
and when I finished
filled it again.
I remember the gravy,
its odor of garlic and celery,
and sopping it up
with pieces of bread.

And now
I taste it again.
The meat of memory.
The meat of no change.
I raise my fork in praise,
and I eat.

THE HOUSE IN FRENCH VILLAGE

for Elizabeth Bishop

It stood by itself
in a sloping field,
it was white
with green
shutters and trim,

and its gambrel roof
gave it the look
of a small
prim barn.
From the porch

when the weather was clear,
I could see Fox Point,
across the bay
where the fishermen,
I was told,

laid out
their catch of tuna
on the pier
and hacked away with axes
at the bellies

of the giant fish.
I would stare
at Wedge Island
where gulls wheeled
in loud broken rings

above their young;
at Albert Hubley's shack
built over water, and sagging;
at Boutelier's wharf
loaded down

with barrels of brine
and nets to be mended.
I would sit
with my grandmother,
my aunt, and my mother,

the four of us rocking
an chairs, watching
the narrow dirt road
for a sign
of the black

baby Austin
my father would drive
to town and back.
But the weather
was not often clear

and all we could see
were sheets of cold rain
sweeping this way and that,
riffling the sea's coat
of deep green,

and the wind
beating the field flat,
sending up to the porch

gusts of salt spray
that carried

the odor of fish
and the rot,
so it seemed,
of the whole bay,
while we kept watch.

THE GARDEN

for Robert Penn Warren

It shines in the garden,
in the white foliage of the chestnut tree,
in the brim of my father's hat
as he walks on the gravel.

In the garden suspended in time
my mother sits in a redwood chair;
light fills the sky,
the folds of her dress,
the roses tangled beside her.

And when my father bends
to whisper in her ear,
when they rise to leave
and the swallows dip and dart
and the moon and stars
have drifted off together, it shines.

Even as you lean over this page,
late and alone, it shines; even now
in the moment before it disappears.

SNOWFALL

Watching snow cover the ground, cover itself,
cover everything that is not you, you see
it is the downward drift of light
upon the sound of air sweeping away the air,
it is the fall of moments into moments, the burial
of sleep, the down of winter, the negative of night.

IV

Night Pieces

NIGHT PIECES

for Bill and Sandy Bailey

I

(after Dickens)

A fine bright moon and thousands of stars!
It is a still night, a very still night
and the stillness is everywhere.

Not only is it a still night
on deserted roads and hilltops
where the dim, quilted countryside seems to doze
as it fans out into clumps of trees dark and unbending
against the sky, with the gray dust of moonlight upon them,

not only is it a still night
in backyards overgrown with weeds, and in woods,
and by tracks where the rat sleeps under the garnet-crusted rock,
and in the abandoned station that reeks of mildew and urine,
and on the river where the oil slick rides the current
sparkling among islands and scattered weirs,

not only is it a still night
where the river winds through marshes and mudflats fouled
by bottles, tires and rusty cans, and where it narrows
through the sloping acres of higher ground covered with plots
cleared and graded for building,

not only is it a still night
wherever the river flows, where houses cluster in small towns,
but farther down where more and more bridges are reflected in it,

where wharves, cranes, warehouses, make it black and awful,
where it turns from those creaking shapes and mingles with the sea,

and not only is it a still night
at sea and on the pale glass of the beach
where the watcher stands upright in the mystery and motion of his life
and sees the silent ships move in from nowhere he has ever been,
crossing the path of light that he believes runs only to him,

but even in this stranger's wilderness of a city
it is a still night. Steeples and skyscrapers grow
more ethereal, rooftops crowded with towers and ducts
lose their ugliness under the shining of the urban moon;
street noises are fewer and are softened, and footsteps
on the sidewalks pass more quietly away.

In this place where the sound of sirens never ceases
and people move like a ghostly traffic from home to work and home,
and the poor in their tenements speak to their gods
and the rich do not hear them, every sound is merged,
this moonlit night, into a distant humming, as if
the city, finally, were singing itself to sleep.

II

(after Carlos Drummond de Andrade)

It is night. I feel it is night
not because darkness has fallen
(what do I care about darkness falling)
but because down in myself the shouting
has stopped, has given up.
I feel we are night,
that we sink into dark

and dissolve into night.
I feel it is night in the wind,
night in the sea, in the stone,
in the harp of the angel who sings to me.
And turning on lights wouldn't help,
and taking my hand wouldn't help. Not now.
It is night where Jess lies down,
where Phil and Fran are asleep,
night for the Simics, night for the Baileys,
night for Dan, for Richard, for Sandy.
For all my friends it is night,
and in all my friends it is night.
It is night, not death, it is night
filling up sleep without dreams,
without stars. It is night,
not pain or rest, it is night,
the perfection of night.
It is night that changes

now in the first glimpse of day,
in the ribbons of rising light,
and the world assembles itself once more.
In the park someone is running,
someone is walking his dog.
For whatever reason, people are waking.
Someone is cooking, someone
is bringing *The Times* to the door.
Streets are filling with light.
My friends are rubbing the sleep from their eyes.
Jules is rubbing the sleep from her eyes,
and I sit at the table
drinking my morning coffee.
All that we lost at night is back.

Thank you, faithful things!
Thank you, world!
To know that the city is still there,
that the woods are still there,
and the houses, and the humming of traffic
and the slow cows grazing in the field;
that the earth continues to turn
and time hasn't stopped,
that we come back whole
to suck the sweet marrow of day,
thank you, bright morning,
thank you, thank you!

Acknowledgments

Sources of the quotations used in The Monument *are listed here
by section and in the order in which they appear in each section.*

2 "The Old Poem" by Octavio Paz.
From *Eagle* or *Sun?*, translated by
Eliot Weinberger. Copyright © 1976
by Octavio Paz and Eliot Weinberger.
Reprinted by permission of New
Directions Publishing Corporation.

3 "The Secret of Life" by Miguel de
Unamuno. From *The Agony of Chris-
tianity and Essays on Faith,* translated
by Anthony Kerrigan. Copyright ©
1974 by Princeton University Press.
Volume 5 of *The Selected Works of
Miguel de Unamuno,* Bollingen Series
LXXXV. Reprinted with permission of
Princeton University Press.
"Nuances of a Theme by Williams" by
Wallace Stevens. From *The Collected
Poems of Wallace Stevens.* Copyright
© 1954 by Wallace Stevens. Reprinted
by permission of Alfred A. Knopf, a
division of Random House, Inc.

4 Sonnet Number 3 by William Shake-
speare.
"Letter to a Friend" by Sir Thomas
Browne. From *The Prose of Sir
Thomas Browne,* edited by Norman
Endicott and Kathleen Endicott (Dou-
bleday, a division of Random House,
Inc., New York).
"The Secret of Life" by Miguel de
Unamuno, translated by Anthony Ker-
rigan. Copyright © 1974 by Princeton
University Press. Volume 5 of *The
Selected Works of Miguel de Una-
muno,* Bollingen Series LXXXV.
Reprinted with permission of Prince-
ton University Press.

6 *The Seagull* by Anton Chekhov.
Thus Spoke Zarathustra by
Friedrich Nietzsche.
"Colder Fire" by Robert Penn Warren.
From *Selected Poems 1923–1975.*
Copyright © 1955 by Robert Penn
Warren. Reprinted by permission of
Random House, Inc.

8 Sonnet Number 101 by William
Shakespeare.

9 "The Man with the Blue Guitar" by
Wallace Stevens. From *The Collected
Poems of Wallace Stevens.* Copyright
© 1954 by Wallace Stevens. Reprinted
by permission of Alfred A. Knopf, a
division of Random House, Inc.

15 "Hydriotaphia or Urne Buriall" by
Sir Thomas Browne. From *The Prose
of Sir Thomas Browne,* edited by Nor-
man Endicott and Kathleen Endicott
(Doubleday, a division of Random
House, Inc., New York).

18 "Song of Myself" by Walt Whitman.
"I Am Not I" by Juan Ramón
Jiménez. From *Lorca and Jiménez:
Selected Poems,* translated by Robert
Bly (Beacon Press, Boston, 1973).
Copyright © 1973 by Robert Bly. Re-
printed by permission of Robert Bly.
In Praise of Darkness by Jorge Luis
Borges, translated by Norman
Thomas di Giovanni. Copyright ©
1969, 1970, 1971, 1972, 1973, 1974
by Emece Editores S.A. and Norman
Thomas di Giovanni. Reprinted by
permission of E. P. Dutton & Com-
pany, Inc.

19 "Death Is a Dream" by M. Playa.

21 *The Fall into Time* by E. M. Cioran, translated by Richard Howard. Copyright © 1964 Editions Gallimard, translation copyright © 1970 Quadrangle Books. Reprinted by permission.

22 "The Twelve Caesars (Nero)" by Suetonius. From *Suetonius,* translated by Robert Graves. Copyright © 1957 by Robert Graves. Reprinted by permission of Allen Lane, The Penguin Press.

25 *Edmond Jaloux* by Yanette Deletang-Tardif.

30 "The Prelude" (Book XIII) by William Wordsworth.
The Gospel According to St. Mark, 13:37.

37 "Essay upon Epitaphs" by William Wordsworth.
"Letter to a Friend" by Sir Thomas Browne. From *The Prose of Sir Thomas Browne,* edited by Norman Endicott and Kathleen Endicott (Doubleday, a division of Random House, Inc., New York).

38 "Sad Strains of a Gay Waltz" by Wallace Stevens. From *The Collected Poems of Wallace Stevens.* Copyright © 1954 by Wallace Stevens. Reprinted by permission of Alfred A. Knopf, a division of Random House, Inc.

47 "Spin from Your Entrails" by Miguel de Unamuno. From *The Agony of Christianity and Essays on Faith,* translated by Anthony Kerrigan. Copyright © 1974 by Princeton University Press. Volume 5 of *The Selected Works of Miguel de Unamuno,* Bollingen Series LXXXV. Reprinted with permission of Princeton University Press.
"A Noiseless Patient Spider" by Walt Whitman.

50 Anonymous Greek poem, translated by W. H. D. Rouse. From *An Anthology of Greek Poetry in Translation.* Copyright © 1937 by W. H. D. Rouse. Reprinted by permission of Oxford University Press.
"Hydriotaphia or Urne Buriall" by Sir Thomas Browne.

52 *Thus Spoke Zarathustra* by Friedrich Nietzsche.
"O Living Always, Always Dying" by Walt Whitman.

A Note About the Author

Mark Strand was born in Summerside, Prince Edward Island, Canada, and was raised and educated in the United States. He has written nine books of poems, which have brought him many honors and grants, including a MacArthur Fellowship and the 1999 Pulitzer Prize for his book of poems *Blizzard of One*. He was chosen as Poet Laureate of the United States in 1990. He is the author of a book of stories, *Mr. and Mrs. Baby,* several volumes of translations (of works by Rafael Alberti and Carlos Drummond de Andrade, among others), the editor of a number of anthologies, and author of two monographs on contemporary artists. He teaches in the Committee on Social Thought at the University of Chicago.

A Note on the Type

The text of this book was set in Sabon, a typeface designed by Jan Tschichold (1902–1974), the well-known German typographer. Based loosely on the original designs by Claude Garamond (c. 1480–1561), Sabon is unique in that it was explicitly designed for hot-metal composition on both the Monotype and Linotype machines, as well as for film setting. Designed in 1966 in Frankfurt, Sabon was named for the famous Lyons punch cutter Jacques Sabon, who is thought to have brought some of Garamond's matrices to Frankfurt.

Composed by NK Graphics, Keene, New Hampshire
Printed and bound by Edwards Brothers,
Ann Arbor, Michigan
Designed by Anthea Lingeman